A Girl Called Dolly Part 2: Life in England

A Girl Called Dolly Part 2: Life in England

SHOBHA SRIVASTAVA

Text Shobha Srivastava and Helen Aitchison, on behalf of StoryTerrace

First print June 2023

CONTENTS

1. FROM INDIA TO ENGLAND

I was born in August 1933 in India, one of six children, to my parents. For many years, there were just three of us, me and two siblings. I was the second oldest, with my elder sister, Vina, being one year older. Along with my brother, the three of us were close growing up. We were affectionately assigned nicknames by my grandfather: I was Dolly, my sister was referred to as Baby and our brother, Billy. I was almost an adult before my further three siblings came along.

My childhood was happy, albeit times were often challenging. I was educated at an English-speaking school and my role-model father worked hard as a doctor in our community before working in the army.

After battling typhoid as a child, I became aware of the determination within me. A determination inspired by my father and a determination I still have to this day, at almost 90 years old.

I enjoyed education and studied hard in India, dedicating myself to my personal development and my early dream of entering the medical field, inspired by my beloved father. Ambition allowed me to decide I wanted to practise as an anaesthetist and I committed to my studies, excelling through exams and eventually securing work in my chosen profession.

I met my husband, Munnoo, at the age of 20. He was seven years older and pursued me, although at the time I was unaware! But eventually, I noticed his affection and we fell in love, got married and began our family.

My career in the medical field had commenced and I worked in physiology before going into teaching when my children were young. Teaching gave me the flexibility that practising medicine could not, allowing me to spend time with my children. Whilst teaching, I had set shifts and working hours, something practising medicine could not guarantee due to changing shift patterns and demands. Practising medicine was my passion, but at the time it was not feasible and teaching medicine was an alternative. During this time, my brother-in-law and his wife also had small children. My mother-in-law could not manage five young grandchildren, even though my oldest daughter was like a little mother to the younger children and was very nurturing.

So teaching it was. I loved teaching; it was not the same as practising medicine, but it was still a job that I enjoyed and was good at. My students appreciated me and saw me as an expert in the field. Many of the students I taught went on to practise medicine here in England.

However, in 1972, a seed began to grow in my mind as I started to think about a potential move to England. After discussing the possibility with Munnoo, we knew it would be a big challenge, but it felt like the right thing to do. By this point, my work in India had reached a barrier that I felt was politically and personally problematic for me. There were issues with my job in India that I knew could not be overcome, leaving me at a crossroads with life-changing decisions to make. I felt there was bribery and corruption in India in the department I was working in, with no signs of it being addressed and resolved. At the time, my superior expected payment for promotion, which went against everything I stood for. I had been brought up to be honest, a quality I prided myself on. I had worked hard and deserved to continue to excel in my profession on merit and not through unscrupulous means. These ongoing issues and incidents led me to explore and seriously consider England as an option for work.

I was respected by my students and dedicated time to keeping up to date with research, publications and practice so that I could share it with my learners. I loved teaching physiology, it is the basis of any other science that comes later, including anaesthesia. I knew my topic and I taught it very well, but securing permanent jobs and promotions in the organisation was not an equal process. This was the sad reality, and I knew I had to take back some control.

In the year of 1972, I had an interview for the permanent lecture role in physiology. I was already teaching on a temporary basis, and a further three people had temporary roles like myself. Interviews were conducted to recruit for numerous permanent lecturer roles in the field, so we all hoped that each of us would secure a position. However, it transpired that many external candidates were shortlisted for interviews and were subsequently offered the jobs, leaving us without permanent positions. It felt unfair and wrong. The difficulties I was having in obtaining a permanent lecture post were eventually investigated by the vice-chancellor; this was due to external interviewers feeling there had been internal bias against me from my superior. He had brought up petty excuses for not hiring me because I was not prepared to be manipulated into paying for a promotion and I would not tolerate corruption.

There was casteism in India, which was another form of racism. I am from the caste which is defined as being the most educated. However, the hierarchy's top caste is the pandits, who are not necessarily the most educated people. My superior wanted to employ a pandit and not myself.

The vice chancellor, in his exploration, stated that the best person deserved to get the job – and that was me. I was therefore given the job which I deserved. I was a good lecturer and was liked by my colleagues and students. However, the issues continued and it became increasingly difficult. I could not get the job I ultimately wanted, which was in anaesthetics.

After exploring options to move to England, I began to realistically plan for the transition from India to living in the UK. Things began to progress and I was scheduled to leave for England after Christmas 1974. During the Christmas holidays, I visited Delhi to obtain my work visa, visitor's visa, etc. It wasn't without challenge, but I was determined as ever. At that time and on so many occasions since, I have thought of what my dear father used to say: 'Nothing is easy for her, but she manages.' He said this many times over the years, from when I was extremely poorly with typhoid as a youngster through to adulthood. I was determined, and I inherited that determination from my father, who was such a wonderful, resilient man.

'There is nothing in the world that you cannot do if you put your heart and soul into it,' was another saying Dad used to repeat. He was right, and he instilled the willpower and ambition in me that I have displayed all my life. I am forever thankful for that. I repeat this phrase to my family, even to this day.

I kept those phrases and Dad's positive attitude in my mind whilst trying to get to England. The General Medical Council wanted my original documents for my registration, so I sent all of these to them. However, I didn't get the documents back promptly. Everything was delayed due to Christmas, but time was not on our side. Still, I continued, having had to obtain copies – and the originals eventually arrived as I was about to leave India.

At last, I was ready to leave India for England. I remember a passenger on the flight who displayed such kindness to me. A stranger who became a friend. We were sitting next to one another and got chatting on the long journey. After much talking and the lady finding out about my circumstances, she invited me to stay with her and her husband until I secured accommodation.

It was so kind of her, despite my initial concerns about this being too good to be true! The money I was allowed to bring over from India wouldn't stretch far. I only had £20. Even in 1975, that was a tiny amount for managing accommodation, travel, food and clothing until I secured employment. I gratefully accepted the offer from the kind lady and I have never forgotten her generosity. When I arrived in England, in the first week of January 1975, I was almost 42 years old.

I was the first person in both my family and my husband's family to come to England. It was a new experience for me and for all of us. I was educated in a convent school during the British time and my father was in the army, so we were close with British families. Even in India, it felt as though my life had a great deal of influence from England. However, it was still a new country, even if it was less alien to me than it could have been, travelling such a long way and into a different culture. Determination came into my body once again, pumping around like blood, and all that my father had instilled in me shone.

It was the weekend when I arrived in England; I rested on the Sunday. I had a few students already in London whom I had taught and who knew I would be arriving. One such student kindly brought me a copy of the British Medical Journal magazine, which featured job vacancies. There was a job advertised in Slough. I was interested but decided to visit the hospital and try to talk to someone. On Monday morning, I travelled to the hospital to meet with the consultant, Richard Jack. I've never forgotten him; he was an essential assistance to me in building my career in the way I wanted. After just a conversation with Richard, he told me he was going to cancel the interviews and offered me the job there and then.

Despite my qualifications in India, I had to begin work at the level of a senior house officer. This was due to England not recognising certain Indian qualifications. However, I was quite pleased with this as I had not practised anaesthetics for a long time; starting at a lower level meant I could ensure I had a refresher of the practice. The job was only temporary and at the bottom of the medical ladder, but it was a start and I embraced the opportunity. Although I was qualified above this grade, I would have to follow the English medical promotion pathway, which meant more training and exams. I did not have an issue with this as I enjoyed the study and, of course, I adored my discipline, wanting to be the best I could be for my patients and my own development.

Accommodation was provided in this role to ensure rapid response to emergencies. This was perfect for me and I transitioned straight to the hospital accommodation to start my new role as a senior house officer.

I was grateful for the opportunity in Slough as this was my stepping stone into a medical career in London. Richard and I got on very well. He appreciated my expertise and professional approach. Due to my experience and knowledge, Richard often had me with him on the operating lists. He was encouraging and excellent at his practice, and I was thankful to be part of his work and to learn from him.

One of the things I taught people was an anaesthetic technique called spinal anaesthetic. This involved using the same drug as an epidural but with a lower dose being administered into the spinal fluid itself. In India, we used this for all surgery below the lungs. This was not the case in England, where spinal anaesthesia had fallen into disrepute in the 1950s after a fatality. In India, it was all we used as it was such a cheap form of aesthesia that also provided pain relief. As a result, I was very skilled and experienced in the process and Richard requested I use it where needed; I even taught him the process.

Slough, although only a short, locum role of around 6-8 weeks, was a positive experience. I met many wonderful people and so many appreciative patients. However, there were also negatives – and the majority of these centred around racism.

Although I came to England in 1975, I could not apply for a passport for five years. Munnoo, my husband, used to come to England, often staying for a maximum of six months. Anything longer was prohibited due to his not being a British resident. Munnoo would try and fit this in around the needs of the children, such as schooling and exams. Often, it meant he spent the winter here, having to tolerate the cold of England. The children remained in India as we did not want to disrupt their schooling and routine at such a critical age. However, I would return every year to India to spend time with the children and my wider family.

It was a challenging time, but we were determined to make a better life for us all. It was a massive transition for each of us, in so many ways. Leaving my children was the most painful thing I had experienced, but Munnoo and I both felt that we would all be reunited permanently at some point soon, in England, as a family. We were strong and adapted, and Munnoo was a magnificent father and a wonderful, supportive husband.

Our grand daughter Sukriti at age 4 with grand dad.

Brothers and Sisters

2. MEDICINE AND MAKING A HOME

Given my role in Slough was a temporary position, I continued to search for permanent jobs. Manchester appealed to me and I soon found a vacancy in the city. It was August 1975 and the position was at Crumpsall Hospital, as it was known at the time, later becoming North Manchester General Hospital. After applying for the role and interviewing, I was offered the job. I was grateful to Richard for his glowing reference of my capabilities. At the time, the hospital struggled to recruit anaesthetists, yet it was all I wanted to practise. It felt like a perfect opportunity for me.

From day one in Manchester, I was made to feel very welcome. The staff team were appreciative that I was filling a much-needed role and I was delighted to have secured a position I wanted. People used to jokingly say that, because I liked to talk, I liked the patient not to talk! However, before they were rendered temporarily mute, unable to talk with anaesthesia, I always took the time to get to know my patients. It was important, even if we only had a few minutes spare, to discover their beliefs and anxieties and ensure I explained the process clearly and thoroughly. It was absolutely essential. My role, after all, was to alleviate their concerns. It brought comfort to the patients. I simply treated them as I would wish to be treated in their circumstances. Anaesthesia was second nature to me, but it wasn't to patients. They needed to feel reassured.

I recall a patient in Manchester who was extremely frightened. The young man had suffered an accident, resulting in a fractured leg that required an operation as his fibula and tibia had moved. Three medical professionals had tried to get a needle into him, without success. The patient was far too nervous, shaking with anxiety and fear. The irony was, the needle would administer sedative drugs to calm him down, but he was too frightened at the thought of it going into his arm. I had learnt to put needles in, but I had not practised the administration for many years. I chatted with this man and tried to put him at ease. I discreetly changed the subject from the actual procedure and did not go into the room and try to insert the needle into him immediately. We chatted – just some small talk – and it began to work, distracting the man but also comforting him as he began to calm down. Finding an interest always worked well to help relax patients and ease their anxiety. I would often talk about football with young boys and men. It helped them to feel calmer and helped me get to know them a little as one of my patients. It was essential to show care for patients and this was a way of doing that.

I was in Manchester for three years in total and very much enjoyed my time there. During my time in north Manchester, I studied and passed the part one exam of the Fellow of Faculty of Anaesthesia of Royal College of Surgeons. This could be taken in London or Dublin, and I travelled to Dublin for the course. I attended and passed, having worked very hard for it. I had to work for two years before I could take the final exam.

I spent a total of one and a half years at North Manchester General Hospital before an opportunity arose at South Manchester General Hospital, Withington Hospital. I applied for the job and I was successful. This was another good hospital, with great colleagues and teaching. Again, I lived on-site, which was needed as a registrar.

After finishing my registrar studies, I began applying for jobs as a senior registrar. It was the natural next step in my career and I was confident I would secure a position due to my skills and references.

The position of the senior registrar in Manchester would be a rotating post, working across the area in a range of hospitals before deciding on a specialism I wished to practise as a consultant. My interest had always been general anaesthesia, but I was aiming to work in obstetrics and gynaecology. This was because I had suffered myself during labour, but also it was an area of interest to me due to the importance of anaesthesia in childbirth and the impact on the mother and baby. At this point, I had still not performed an epidural, although I had been taught how to. This had been the choice of anaesthesia for longer operations as opposed to childbirth. I became very interested in the procedure and hoped it would be my focus in the near future.

During my time in Manchester, Munnoo continued to travel to visit me in England and I would return with him to India. This was usually in December or January. I would stay with my family in India for several weeks, using my annual leave allowance before returning to England. It was always so wonderful to see my family and share stories of what we were all doing. The time there was precious and it made my return to England harder each time. However, I stayed strong and determined, knowing that this was for the best for us all. The distance between us all never diluted the love we had as a family.

I remained in Manchester until 1977 when I moved to London, where I stayed until 1979. I really enjoyed Manchester; it was a nice place and I felt valued. However, I felt there were limited options open at the time for me to progress. I would have remained in Manchester longer had I been able to secure a promotion. In 1977, I secured a job at East Ham Memorial Hospital, London. At this time there was unrest in Uganda as Idi Amin, the president of Uganda, attempted to force Asians out of the country – many of whom were seeking refuge in London. This led to an increase in racism in the area, which I was a victim of on several occasions.

In Manchester, if colleagues of an ethnic minority mentioned racist incidents, it shocked me. The people were so nice and I had not experienced such hate from patients and the public. Munnoo also loved Manchester and felt accepted and happy there. However, London felt so different and it made me wish I was back in Manchester.

One time in London I was assaulted in a park by two girls shouting racist slurs and abuse at me. Another disturbing incident that I will never forget happened when Munnoo was in London with me. I used to get one day a week off, and one particular week when Munnoo was here he wanted to visit Dagenham. We didn't drive as driving in London was not appealing; even back then it was manic on the roads. I always used public transport or walked where I could, and it worked well for us both to get out and about. On this particular day, we were coming back from the day out in Dagenham, waiting at a bus stop to travel home. Around 20 people were waiting at the bus stop alongside us, and more people were over the road, waiting for the arrival of the bus travelling in the opposite direction. As we stood there waiting, four people approached us and asked if we could tell them the time. Munnoo checked his watch. As soon as he looked away, they took advantage and pounced on him, attacking him out of nowhere. Elbows, fists and feet, all went towards Munnoo, assaulting him as he stood helpless and I stood by him, screaming for them to stop. Munnoo tried to get out of the way of the assaults, but there were so many of them against him.

All of the people at the bus stop failed to intervene despite the brutal attack happening right in front of their eyes. I could not comprehend how another human could stay still and watch such a brutal attack. There wasn't just one person watching, there were multiple people standing there not helping as my husband was physically assaulted. I wasn't sure if this was out of fear or racism.

I was screaming for help, for someone to stop this barrage of assaults against my husband. I was terrified that they would kill Munnoo. Time seemed to stop as the violence went on and on – until I heard a car screech to a stop. The perpetrators ran away, possibly thinking that the car belonged to the police. Munnoo was left with a mess of injuries. A man got out of the car and came towards us. He had seen from a distance what had been happening. He looked at the group of people still standing at the bus stop. The people who had not assisted us in our moments of need, moments that seemed to go on forever as I became more and more worried about Munnoo.

The man said loudly, with contempt, to all the people that were at the bus stop, 'No one moved to help this good gentleman.' He looked at us both, sympathetically, and told us to sit in his car so we could report the incident to the police. I asked the kind man to drive us to the hospital I worked at. He did so and Munnoo was treated. He received injections and had stitches in 10-15 places on the back of his body; many bruises formed across his skin.

Munnoo healed and the physical injuries from that vicious attack were repaired. However, he did not go out for almost six months, instead saying that he wanted to stay in. The abuse he was victim to on that day mentally scarred him and the psychological impact took a long time to heal, much longer than the physical wounds. London was never the same for us both and I wanted away from the place.

One positive in London was that I did make some new friends. It was more challenging as I felt I could always be categorised as one of the groups of people who had come over from Uganda, which increased discrimination, but there were some nice people. Racism was in and out of my work in London. I felt there were comments, processes and views from some members of the medical staff that were discriminatory and eventually it became too much. It was time to move on.

We left London in 1979 for an opportunity in Aldershot. This job came about through a midwife my cousin knew, a lady called Lorina. They worked together in Blackpool. Lorina was coming to London and was going to stay with her niece, Margaret, who was an army wife. We went to meet with Lorina and Margaret, along with Margaret's husband, David, who was in the army. Munnoo and David got on well, chatting about DIY, and Munnoo offered to help around their home, as he did so generously with many people. We got into a conversation about our careers and I mentioned I was struggling to get a job in anaesthesia. At this, David's back straightened and he almost jumped out of his chair, announcing they needed anaesthetists for the army. This was wonderful for me to hear and I knew it could be a positive route out of London.

David was in admin as a major at this point. He arranged for me to meet with Brigadier Belsham the next day. We had a discussion and I told the brigadier that I wanted a job with the army. There were two options for me. One was to remain in the NHS and the army would request for me to work with the army, or I could join the army itself. I decided on the former and I was offered a senior registrar's job on a consultant's salary. It was perfect! Sadly, David has now passed, but I remain in contact with Margaret and have fond memories of the man who helped me secure this wonderful role.

I joined the team at Aldershot promptly, receiving accommodation in the officers' mess. The experiences I encountered at Aldershot were experiences I believe I could never have obtained in any other post. The patients, the injuries, the whole practice was so different. We had many soldiers coming back injured from Northern Ireland, injuries such as shrapnel wounds right through to head injuries and limb injuries. As well as this, I treated many head injuries resulting from accidents on the M25 which had just been built.

The job in Aldershot was available to me as long as I wanted it and I ended up staying in the role for two years until 1981. The experience enhanced my knowledge and I very much enjoyed my role in Aldershot, but the itch was there for more. One day I saw an advert for a position in South Tyneside in the north of England; I recall that the job was advertised as a 'challenge'. It caught my eye and I thought, *Why not!?*

In 1981, there was a train which ran from Newcastle to Mile End Road in South Tyneside. I caught the train once I arrived in Newcastle and had been advised that, once I reached Mile End Road, I could get a taxi to the hospital where I was to be interviewed. When I arrived at Mile End Road, I asked a local lady for help in locating a taxi. The local woman called me 'love' and made me feel at ease immediately. She helped me get a taxi and told the taxi driver exactly what to charge me – and not a penny more. What a magnificent first impression I received.

At the time, the hospital had sites called the Ingham Infirmary and the District General Hospital. The consultant at the Ingham Infirmary was an inspiring missionary called Anne Seymour, who the block of flats I now live in was named after. She became a great friend of mine and was the first medical colleague I met in South Tyneside.

A room had been arranged for me at Ingham Infirmary for the night I arrived, then I would be interviewed the following day. I remember arriving at Mile End Road and experiencing a feeling that consumed me. It was the feeling of being home; it was as if I was absolutely meant to be here. It was overwhelmingly wonderful and I knew at once that South Tyneside was the place for me – so much so that the feeling I had been here before niggled away at me, despite my lack of belief in previous lives.

I had my interview the following day at the next-door building, the General Hospital. For the first time in my interviewing experience, there were many candidates short-listed for the interview – around eight. There had been previous issues at the hospital and they had been relying on locums. There was an Egyptian doctor called Eliot Dayan, who was a magnificent practitioner and became a treasured friend. Despite the competition of the candidates being interviewed, I was successful in securing the job.

I didn't have to think. I knew that not only did I want the job, but I also wanted to live in South Tyneside. In particular, I wanted to live in the town I had arrived in, South Shields, in a way I had never felt during all my travels within England. When I told Munnoo, he questioned why I wanted to live in this unknown town on the northeast coast of England. When he eventually visited, Munnoo also thought there was something rather special about South Tyneside.

And so my new life in South Shields began in August 1981, on my birthday!

TYNE AND WEAR
DIVERSITY
AWARDS

3. SETTLING IN SOUTH SHIELDS, NORTH EAST ENGLAND

When my life in South Tyneside started in 1981, I was warned that the role of consultant at South Tyneside General Hospital would be a challenge. I was their first female doctor and there had been a large gap of time between my appointment and the departure of the former consultant following his retirement. The hospital had struggled to find the right person for the role and it meant that much work was needed. When my role commenced, the Clinical Quality Commission (CQC) had issues with South Tyneside Hospital. The hospital had locums and not consultants, which meant they did not have the required staff to train junior medical professionals. Hard work was needed to stabilise, rectify and improve the service. I felt I was the person to do exactly that. I lived three minutes drive away from the hospital. Whilst my colleagues lived in an affluent part of the town, my priority was being able to access the hospital promptly in case of emergencies. I did just that on many occasions – and sometimes when other colleagues were on call and should have been responding.

When I came to South Tyneside General, I aimed to develop the service. The service had been neglected for so long due to inconsistent staff and needed attention and progression. As anaesthetics, we were able to explore epidurals, pain management clinics and intensive care clinics. My idea was to employ a consultant to lead the pain management and likewise a consultant to lead the intensive care clinics. I would lead the epidurals and oversee the team as a whole.

The first step was to advertise, and we were able to recruit for the two positions. It wasn't always plain sailing, however, and one of the appointees was not the easiest person to get on with, nor was he the most professional, on one occasion referring to me as 'Hitler'.

There were so many times we had patients that were touch-and-go at the hospital, on the brink of life and death. In my position, I was a doctor before anything else, even sometimes before being a human. Medicine was in my blood, my soul, and I always took my job with 100% pride, dedication and commitment, even down to where I chose to live. The house I bought in South Shields was on a newly-built estate. It was a lovely house and for me, ideal, being only three minutes away from the hospital. When I was on call, I didn't put my car in the garage. This meant a saving of time if I had to get to the hospital quickly in one of the many life-and-death situations. I could get from my house to the hospital in three minutes. I remember a time that I wasn't on call and my colleague was. He had not been picking up the emergency calls and the medical team on shift called me. I answered and promptly got to the hospital, despite my car being in the garage. I got there just in time to help deliver a baby who was at risk of death.

The maternity patients were always memorable. Mother with baby or babies getting ready to enter the world. It was wonderful and I used to get mothers coming up to me in town reminding me I delivered their baby, including when their baby was certainly no longer a baby and in fact an adult! It always made me smile and I was delighted that I could be part of such a memorable event in a parent's life, as well as ease what can also be such a stressful, anxiety-filled time. Patients told me how they remembered my kindness and calmness and the support I showed them.

I started the process of epidurals on the maternity ward at South Tyneside General. Before this, women in labour used to have to go to Sunderland Royal or Newcastle RVI for this procedure if they had prolonged labour. After this was implemented in South Tyneside General, our maternity unit became one of the best and we excelled with our CQC inspections and awards.

Another wonderful thing about South Shields was that there was so little racism. People believed Indian doctors were good and respected us. My colleagues, my patients and the community were all kind, decent people.

For all the positive things that happened in South Tyneside, I will never forget a tragedy that occurred. I lost a patient on the table who should not have died. Death happens during hospital procedures and is more likely with certain patients. For example, if a very elderly person comes in for an operation and has many underlying conditions, they are more likely to die. However, it should not happen to a patient who has no conditions and seems fit and healthy. One unforgettable, tragic day, it happened to one such patient of mine.

The patient was a man who was 67 years old, with a family, who had never experienced any significant illness in his life. Nor had he needed any operations in his life. He came to the hospital with a broken hip that needed attention. I was working with one of the best surgeons we had at the hospital on the day, named Tony, along with an experienced theatre assistant. The patient needed a hip replacement. The theatre assistant would ensure that the right amount of anaesthesia was ready to use, based on each patient's weight. I would always double-check and help out and I did that day.

We began the procedure for the patient as we did on a daily basis, which included administering the needle, drip and medication, then ensuring ventilation with oxygen to support breathing before inserting the tube and starting the anaesthetic. My teacher in India used to reiterate the importance of watching your patient and touching your patient. Looking, feeling and touching to ensure the patient is OK. I was observing my patient and could see that he was going blue. I asked for help; the pulse was not there. The stethoscope indicated no heartbeat, so we began cardiac massage. All the time I was wondering what had happened. We could not revive the patient and the surgeon came into the operating room. He opened the patient’s chest to massage his heart with his own hands. However, we could not save the patient and he died.

The patient’s death became a coroner's case because it was an unexplained death. I was pleased about this as I also wanted to know what had happened. We did not have knowledge of any underlying medical conditions or problems with this patient. I had chatted with him and nothing had been identified, including no allergies, no health concerns and no previous operations or illnesses. I was baffled and disturbed by the case and I wanted answers. There was a wait for the case to go to court. However, the day after the patient's death I was alerted by a friend to a story in the local newspaper, the *Shields Gazette*. I purchased a copy of the newspaper and saw the story about the case.

'Young looking Indian doctor kills our dad' was the headline.

I was devastated and eager for the case to get to the coroner's court so we could explore what had happened in this tragedy. This would determine if something had happened that would constitute negligence. Usually, this would be if the patient had not been oxygenated enough or had been administered the wrong drug, for example. We knew that had not happened and therefore I could simply not understand how the patient had died. We all wanted answers. It was an upsetting time, and my superior, Tony, was very supportive. He sat me down and gave me time, reiterating that I was an experienced, skilled anaesthetist and that these things do happen. However, it had never happened to me before and I was distressed for the family of the patient. I also sought support from another anaesthetist in another hospital based in Newcastle, to chat through what had happened. The conversation and support were invaluable.

I recall going into crown court that day to give evidence and seeing the family there. I shall never forget the faces of the family of the deceased. The patient's children and wife were sitting in the court, and as I walked past to take the stand there was such contempt on their faces. It was horrific. I understood: they wanted someone to blame. They wanted an explanation and they were grieving. I took the stand and told the truth, as I always had and always have since. My colleagues and I all gave evidence on that day. I wasn't sure what was going to happen or what the outcome would be. However, I was prepared to take any outcome aimed at myself as a professional, even if that included being struck off as a doctor.

It transpired through the coroner's exploration and evidence that it was likely the patient had died as a result of an allergy that had never been discovered, likely due to the patient's lack of previous operations and illnesses. The coroner concluded that this would have been why the patient's heart suddenly stopped, and he thanked me and the team for conducting the correct procedures. There was nothing more we could have done.

This was bittersweet. Ultimately, a man – a patient – had still died. I remember the faces of the family appearing less filled with blame against me once the verdict was announced. I hope time helped them heal a little from a tragedy that no one could have pre-empted.

The medical world can produce such wonderful, life-enhancing results, but there is always a downside. The good and the bad, the positive and the negative. This was most definitely a very tragic negative. The outcome of the case was documented in the *Gazette*. A small paragraph on the outcome, but it was over. The case remains etched in my mind as if it were yesterday.

During my time at South Tyneside General Hospital, there was a teaching group in South Shields that I became involved with. I always did a lot of reading and kept up to date with my practice. I was invited one time to give a talk and this went well, which resulted in a few more opportunities to share knowledge and practice. Each hospital would have a person dedicated to being a tutor to represent their area to the Royal College. This person would be the link between the college and the hospital. I was appointed the tutor for the hospital, which involved visits to London. It was another part of my career that I very much enjoyed.

Alongside this, I used to go and work in Sweden every year. This experience started in 1978 when I was based in Aldershot and a consultant colleague used to fly out to Sweden each year. One particular year, he was unable to go and asked if I would travel there. Of course, I was always keen on gaining new experiences and I liked to travel, so I happily agreed. Munnoo travelled with me and we both loved Sweden. On our first trip, we went to a place called Lulea, close to the Arctic Circle, the most stunning of locations, where the midnight sun was phenomenal. A spectacular, memorable sight.

For the first few years of visiting Sweden, I continued to work in Lulea. The team were welcoming and I was offered a job there on a few occasions. The patients and the community were also delightful people, and luckily many of the Swedes spoke English, making communication easier. I would go out for around three weeks at a time.

Next, I worked in a place called Norrtalje, close to Stockholm, which was another lovely location. I also spent the odd summer working in Belgium. Working in Sweden was positive for many reasons, including the good money it allowed me to make, which was then spent in the weeks after leaving Sweden, when I would travel back to India for a further three weeks, using up my annual leave. In Sweden, there was also a national health service that worked very well. It was a pleasure to therefore work in a system that was honest, genuine, sincere and hardworking. It chimed with my own values and I thoroughly enjoyed my work in Sweden, being lucky enough to work there each year for many years, up until 1994.

I stayed in my role at South Tyneside General Hospital until I retired in 1998, making it the longest position I held in England. It always felt like the place I simply had to be and I have always said I will only go out of South Tyneside in a box. I have given my everything to this borough and it has been a pleasure. When I retired in 1998, I was aged 65. On my retirement, we had a big party at a local hotel. It was lovely to have all my colleagues, recent and past, there. I have remained in contact with many colleagues over the years. Sadly, some have now passed.

Although my career in medicine had come to an end, it didn't feel like the massive void it could have for other long-serving medical staff, as I had already commenced working more within the community.

In 1992, I established a group called Hindu Nari Sangh, which means Hindu Women's Association. The inspiration for this came after seeing so many doctors' wives struggling with the cultural transition for their children in England. I always held parties at my home for friends in the area. Munnoo would cater for everyone, cooking the most wonderful food, and it felt like a little community in itself, us all coming together to eat and chat. The women would talk about the fact their children did not know about the rich culture of their heritage, as they were growing up in England. It was important that children were aware of their heritage, so I suggested setting up a group enabling us to talk about heritage and culture with the children. The wives felt it was a good idea and we set up an initial meeting at the Brinkburn Centre in South Shields. For that initial meeting, we had over 40 women attending, women from all over Tyne and Wear, not just South Tyneside. At our first meeting, it was pleasing to see so many people, including children. All the women had the same message, that their children had no idea where they came from.

We needed a name, so this was opened to the group. Hindu Nari Sangh was chosen. We started by giving talks to community groups, businesses, etc. I also offered groups in my home and organised meetings at the Brinkburn Centre. Mainly it was me talking, as one of the older women here at the time. I had spent the first 40 years of my life in India and returned each year. But I also had so many years in England. I could see both cultures and felt my experience would support others. It was amazing to have the group but equally as important to raise awareness in the community, in South Tyneside and beyond. I met so many people and felt conversations and talks about culture and heritage helped us become even more understanding as a society.

Something else that was created through Hindu Nari Sangh was the Bollywood dance group that began in 1999. I am still part of it today and we meet weekly. This group originally started as a classical dance group, to represent the traditional, classical dances of each area of India, that originated from the temples. The group proved to be very popular and we still have many women attending, several of whom are white women and older women. It has developed into a group that not only provides dance and exercise but also an opportunity for women to meet, socialise and become friends.

Before I left medicine, I received an invitation from a lady called Vimla Storey. Vimla established Apna Ghar, a minority ethnic women's centre, in South Shields in 1987. She had been a teacher in India and when she moved to South Tyneside, Vimla wanted to continue to teach women, in different ways. Women who had come to England from the Indian subcontinent had very little education, especially those coming from certain areas, such as Bangladesh. It meant that women did not know English, except for the odd word, such as 'OK' or 'Thank you'. Vimla wanted to support these women and therefore set up Apna Ghar, which translates to 'Our Home'. Dr Malik, who at the time was director of public health, and his daughter, Salima Malik, were crucial to getting office space in the early days for Apna Ghar and supporting

Vimla. Dr Malik was on the board and Salima, his daughter, is now on the board.

Apna Ghar became a welcoming place where women could attend and meet other women, making friends and increasing their confidence. Vimla then started running conversation classes that aimed to help women understand English better and build their vocabulary. Soon after, she employed English teachers, and they continue to work within the service today, helping women of all cultures and backgrounds to feel integrated and supported in South Tyneside.

Vimla had invited me to visit Apna Ghar before my retirement. She was keen for me to get involved, but I had advised her that I was unable to commit during that time as I was still working as a doctor. However, the day I retired I received a phone call from Vimla! The next day, in August 1998, I visited Apna Ghar and became part of the team. I joined the board immediately, and in 1999 I was elected chair of the board. I remained in this role until 2020. Even to this day, I am still involved with Apna Ghar and visit frequently. Sadly, Vimla died in 2020, but her work continues to make an impact and her legacy is in the excellent service and valuable support Apna Ghar provides in our society and beyond.

Apna Ghar and Hindu Nari Sangh were about giving women voices. I remember one time I was at one of the Hindu Nari Sangh group meetings on a Friday evening. I noticed a girl there who was changing her clothes and I asked her why. She told me that she was not allowed to wear jeans at home and if her father saw her in them, he would beat her up. She was changing into Bangladeshi clothes to return home. It was very sad to hear about and see this young girl who lived in the Western world but could not dress in such a way.

Once I retired and joined Apna Ghar, the offers of community work continued to come in. It suited me as I liked to keep busy, and not only that, I liked to support and improve our society. At one point, I was on around 10 different boards across the North East. I was very busy, out and about most days of the week. Munnoo used to ask me, 'Have you really retired?' and 'Where are you going today?' But he knew how important my community work was to me and he was proud of everything I dedicated my time to.

Through Apna Ghar and Hindu Nari Sangh, I visited many places and consequently became involved with other services. I was invited to be a governor at Mortimer School, both the primary and the senior schools. I enjoyed these roles and I always aimed to try and get South Tyneside recognised, appreciated and in receipt of the same financial support as the major cities in the area, such as Sunderland and Newcastle. My loyalty to South Tyneside was and still is so strong.

After retiring, I was on the North East Ambulance Service board and also on the Community Foundation of Northumberland and Tyne and Wear board. I became involved with the North East Ambulance Service as people knew me from being a doctor. Once I retired, they invited me to attend some of their meetings and then I became involved in the board. All the boards I was a member of were for services that interested me; it was an easy 'Yes' each time I was asked to participate.

I have been able to help in many developments in South Tyneside which have resulted in much recognition and many awards. The first award I received was the Pride of South Tyneside Award, in 1995. I went on to receive further awards, including the Bangla Award, the North East Ambulance Service award and the Asian Business Connexions' People's Choice Award in 2021, to name a few. In total, I have received around over awards and I am very grateful for all of them.

The most memorable recognition was when I received my MBE from the now King Charles in 2017. It was a magnificent surprise to receive a letter from the late Queen, advising me I had been awarded an MBE. I had no idea who had nominated me; to this day I still don't know. However, it was very bittersweet as I received the letter of notification only a few months after Munnoo died. I wish he had known as he would have been so proud of me. He used to joke with me, asking me, 'Are you a Dame yet?' as though he was almost waiting for royal recognition of my work.

After receiving the letter advising me of my MBE, I was invited to Buckingham Palace. I informed the children and all three were able to attend on the day. It was a phenomenal day and we all enjoyed every minute. The then Prince Charles knew a great deal about India. He showed lots of interest in my story and it was lovely to talk with him and answer his questions about my work.

I thoroughly enjoyed all my board roles. I never missed meetings and I was always prepared; it was the way I worked and I liked the positions. Anywhere that I and other people could do positive work for the community, we did, and many of those services I am no longer a part of continue to thrive in the area. I still have involvement with some minor roles. It keeps me busy and allows me to continue to be part of the community I love so much, here in South Shields.

With our seven grandchildren

4. PRACTICE AND PREJUDICE

Sadly, I have experienced discrimination in my life. This happened both in my career and outside of work, and it was more prevalent in certain areas I worked in. When I came to England, there were pockets of racial discrimination in many areas of the country, as there still are today.

Of course, there are always some individuals and groups of people who will demonstrate discriminatory behaviours in every community, whether this is against skin colour, religion, sexuality, ability or another identifying characteristic, lifestyle or belief. In any part of the world, some communities and some individuals are more accepting and others more prejudiced. That's something that hasn't necessarily changed over the years, but when I came to England, in the mid to late 1970s, I did have experiences of hatred towards me due to my race.

As a woman, I also faced sex discrimination, meaning at times it felt like I was doubly discriminated against. Before I came to England, I had heard about racism, but in a way, I felt I was almost immune from it, perhaps because of speaking English so well and knowing about the Western world. Coming to England felt like such a natural step for me as I had Western influences growing up, which made me feel comfortable with England before I even arrived here.

However, I quickly learnt that my skin colour and race could be the target of bullies, ignorance and cruelty from people.

In London, I found discrimination to be the most prevalent. Given the multi-cultural, diverse communities that are in London, even back all those years ago, it is perhaps surprising. However, the incidents of abuse both in and out of work related to my skin colour were the most offensive I have experienced throughout my life in England.

I remember an incident of racism directed towards me by a patient in London. He was waiting to receive treatment and was becoming increasingly irritable and loud. 'I ain't having no needle from a Paki doctor,' he shouted at me as I tried to help treat him. The consultant at the time had to come and intervene in this incident and advised the patient that I would be giving the anaesthetic or the patient could leave and risk dying. The patient soon changed his attitude and I was grateful that my superior supported me. But it was very unpleasant to be targeted in such a way. I won't ever forget it. Despite being confident, resilient and determined, I was still human.

There was also institutional racism within the NHS, both from colleagues and in the processes for promotion. I found this more prevalent later in my career than in the earlier days, although, of course, it was still there. The difference was that medical teams needed more junior jobs filled, such as senior house officer jobs, so these positions were easier to obtain. It was more difficult to secure a registrar job and almost impossible to acquire a senior registrar job, which would be a stepping stone to a consultant's role. Everywhere I went for a job at a lower position, I got in. This changed with the higher ranking positions and I felt that, despite my qualifications, my experience and my outstanding references, I still had the invisible barrier, which was all too visible to me.

I always performed well during interviews and knew I was excellent at my job. I also had outstanding references, but in some places, I strongly feel my skin colour prevented me from climbing the professional ladder. I felt like the medical world wanted Asian medical colleagues but not in senior roles. This of course wasn't the case everywhere, but I did feel it was the case in some places, including Manchester. Despite working hard every moment of my life and passing my exams, I encountered this prejudice.

Being a woman in medicine in the 1970s and 80s was also a factor. In society in general at this time, women were given less respect, and stereotypes persisted around women in certain roles, especially professional roles. I was the first female anaesthetist at South Tyneside Hospital and therefore the first Indian, female anaesthetist. This could have been the most challenging role regarding possible discrimination, but luckily I never experienced prejudice in South Tyneside.

Discrimination dissolved over time, especially during my time in South Shields. But sadly, it never completely disappears. The messages here and my own, personal experiences are important as racial discrimination and gender discrimination do still exist, even in 2023. Although people are more inclusive, there will always be some level of discrimination where people are involved. However, I hope there are more challenges against the minority of people who hold these views and institutions become better at dealing with prejudice so that people can be employed on credit, commitment and skills as opposed to what they look like, where they are from or what they believe in.

Prejudice and racism clouded some of my practice, but I was able to manage it in my own way. I had support and a determined, resilient nature.

Of course, this does not make it acceptable, and at times it was hurtful and also hindered my career. Some people would struggle with this and people do struggle with discrimination every day, in many ways. I hope in time, as societies become more diverse, that people are more tolerant and inclusive and that merit is based on skills and capability and not on race, religion, skin colour or any other factor.

I want my story to be read as a message to never give up on a dream and your capabilities. Do not let barriers prevent you from walking the path you wish to walk.

up strength sport – breaking cultural stereotypes as a Muslim woman. She was crowned British champion in June last year.

8. Dr Shobha Srivastava MBE
Pioneering medic
Dr Shobha overcame sexism and racism to become one of the UK's first female anaesthetists. Now 88, Dr Shobha lives at McCarthy Stone's Seymour Court development in South Shields, where she dedicates her time to empowering unprivileged women from ethnic minorities.

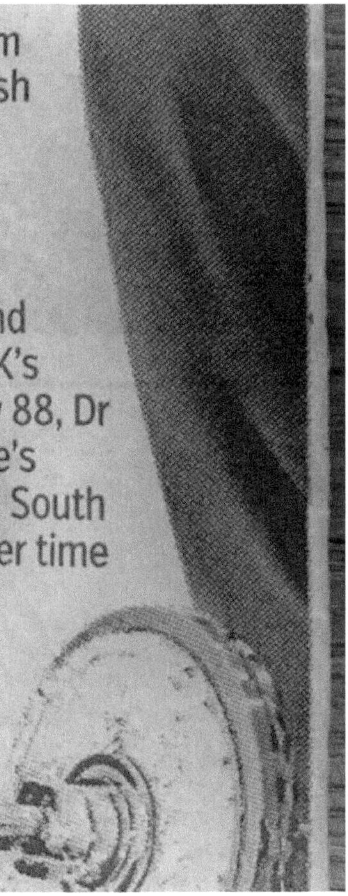

9. Nikki Ross
Supports victims of domestic

Woman's Day, we celebrate
rich, change and save lives

Management and helps young couples prepare for the unexpected.

5. Amanda Parker
Mental health charity founder
Amanda lost her eldest child to suicide in December 2021. She launched HarveyParkerTrust.org to help the mental health and wellbeing of other young creative people who are marginalised.

6. Eva Prendergast
Polar scientist
Even as a schoolgirl Eva, 27, was obsessed with dolphins. The marine mammal specialist heads to Antarctica this year, as Intrepid expedition guide on the Ocean Endeavour in a partnership with WWF.

7. Dr Amna Khan
British champion powerlifter
After a car accident Amna, 41, took up strength sport – breaking cultural stereotypes as a Muslim woman. She was crowned British champion in June last year.

8. Dr Shobha Srivastava MBE
Pioneering medic
Dr Shobha overcame sexism and racism to become one of the UK's first female anaesthetists. Now 88, Dr Shobha lives at McCarthy Stone's Seymour Court development in South Shields, where she dedicates her time to empowering unprivileged women from ethnic minorities.

. Nikki Ross
upports ctims of mestic olence and sexual abuse
mer assistant police stable, single working mum CEO of charity Thames ey Partnership, Nikki, 55, helps victims of estic violence and sexual abuse.

nia Adib
pioneer
qualifying, consultant Tania was d at the lack of options offered to who were forced to accept ting conditions such as vaginal laxity and incontinence and having

ROGER SPOOR AWARD
This award was made by
The High Sheriff of
Tyne & Wear
to
SHOBHA SRIVASTAVA
HINDU NARI SANGH
in recognition of
great and valuable services
to the community
The award also recognises the appreciation of
the residents and people of the said High Sheriff's
County for activity and contribution in
enhancing the life of the community
High Sheriff

8. Dr Shobha Srivastava MBE

Shobna become one of the UK's first female anesthetists (Picture: Dr Shobha Srivastava)

Pioneering medic

Dr Shobha overcame sexism and racism to become one of the UK's first female anesthetists. Now 88, Dr Shobha lives at McCarthy Stone's Seymour Court development in South Shields, where she dedicates her time to empowering unprivileged women from ethnic minorities.

5. LOVE AND LOSS

My father was such a massive influence on my life, as was my grandfather. Dad was such a good man, not only to our community in India as a doctor and within his army service, but also to us as a family. He was a loving husband and father, we could have not wished for more in a role model. He was kind, encouraging and supportive. My father instilled beliefs in me that I carry to this day, but also qualities essential to navigate life and its obstacles. Qualities such as motivation, ambition, honesty and determination. The ability to grow as a person, believe in myself and be kind. He also influenced my decision to go into medicine. He was a magnificent man.

The loss of Dad was profound on myself and my family. Even now when someone close to me passes, I still see my father's face. My father died at the hands of a surgeon and he shouldn't have. I blame myself and it will remain with me until the day I die. My father went into hospital for a routine operation and didn't come out alive. He required a simple operation, an oesophagostomy. In those days, they used aluminium rods, whereas nowadays they are plastic and flexible. These aluminium rods could nick the oesophagus, creating a hole between the oesophagus and the lungs, which led to lung failure. This happened to my father and the surgeon did not accept that this mistake had occurred, which ultimately led to my father's death. Perhaps the surgeon did not accept the issue because he knew me; I had even taught him at one point. This was another example of what I felt was dishonesty and corruption in my birth country and another reason that I wanted to be away from India. I would spend the nights at the hospital with my father as he died. They were precious times and I cherish them still.

Over the years, I have lost many people, including my mother, older sister and, of course, my father. All have been great losses. I also lost my dear husband, Munnoo.

Munnoo was born in 1926 and grew to be a very hard-working and intelligent man. His father wanted him to study medicine, but he was interested in engineering and went to engineering college. However, he did not get the opportunity to complete this study as he was required, as the oldest son, to help out in the family business. His father was an entrepreneur and after establishing a successful furnishing business, set up New India Coffee House. Munnoo began working at the coffee shop and the business was very popular. We used to frequent there in the evenings, at weekends. It was a great place, serving food and drinks in an inviting atmosphere. I would visit New India Coffee House with my friends, and Munnoo noticed me as he worked.

At the time, I did not have the highest degree of confidence. As a child, I was told I was the ugliest and darkest of girls. It damaged my self-esteem greatly and having been so poorly as a youngster also impacted my perception of myself. When Munnoo would come and talk to us, I assumed he was interested in my friend and was just being polite. Another girl told me that Munnoo always seemed to get his chair close to me when he came over to chat. Each time we would go to pay for our food and drinks, we would be advised that the bill had been taken care of. It was paid for by Munnoo. I couldn't believe that any man would ever fall in love with me, so the attention and kindness from Munnoo towards me were not recognised and I assumed his affections were for my friend. Eventually, I realised his affections were aimed at me. Munnoo used to say that he had paid the large bills at New India Coffee House from the visits my friends and I made there, paying for fish and chicken dishes, when all along I was eating only 'grass', referring to my vegetarianism.

Munnoo said to me a few weeks before he died, 'I loved you the moment I set eyes on you and I will love you until the minute I die.'

He was the most loyal, considerate husband, nursing me through all my illnesses and all the operations I have had over the years. He was always by my side, caring for me.

When I moved to England and Munnoo began visiting, he wanted to work in England. All the years he came to England, he wasn't allowed to work due to political decisions and restrictions. When eventually he could work, he was too elderly. However, what he did was learn the trade of DIY and constructed, repaired, replaced and maintained everything in our family home in South Shields. There was nothing he could not turn his hand to and nothing he would not try to learn and master. Not only did he ensure our home was safe, secure and well-maintained, but he also helped in the community, assisting our friends, neighbours and strangers with any DIY needs. He was self-taught and all jobs in our house and outside our house he completed with pride. I remember a time when some of the garages on our estate in South Shields were broken into. Many had been targeted and damaged. Ours hadn't, as Munnoo had previously ensured the safety of the contents with a robust lock. All the neighbours now wanted a lock to protect their garage from attack or repeated attacks by thieves. Munnoo went around our street and fitted locks on all of the garages. He was so kind and radiated community spirit in his thinking.

Munnoo always said to me, when he visited England, that he had never seen me as happy as I was practising medicine here. At times I felt torn; the pull of returning to my family in India was always present, especially in those early years.

When I retired from South Tyneside General Hospital, our family in India and even people in South Shields expected us to return to India for good. However, I had already forged new commitments and goals I wanted to achieve in the community. Just because I was retiring from medicine did not mean I was retiring from my community, a community that was so precious to me.

Then, after Munnoo passed, everyone expected me to return to my roots in India. But for me, I had planted new roots in South Shields. I may not have had Munnoo by my side any longer, but I had friendships and community. I had many roles and important commitments. More than that, I was happy in South Shields, despite losing my husband.

Munnoo became a brilliant cook, despite never cooking in his life until he came to South Tyneside. He was famous for his chicken curry! Munnoo became friends with a retired physician, Manni Anderson, who I met through another colleague, Eliot Dayan. Munnoo and Manni became friends over a shared interest in DIY. We would invite Manni and his wife, Rita, to our home on many occasions, where Munnoo would cook chicken curry. One time, it was another friend's birthday and Munnoo was invited. He was not able to go on the day but made chicken curry for the guests. Manni attended the birthday party and tasted Munnoo's chicken curry. He recognised it straight away! This was a man who had never cooked, yet he had a real talent in the kitchen and made memorable food that was enjoyed by so many. Whilst he was a phenomenal cook, he was not so good at cleaning up! There used to be food splashes all over the kitchen. I didn't mind too much as I was particular about cleaning and ensuring everything was cleansed so that nothing compromised my vegetarianism.

I had a wonderful life with my husband, but sadly he passed in 2016. For around six months before he died he would make comments about not being able to do anything and that there was little point in living. He was 89 years old when he died on 27th February 2016.

He would have reached his 90th birthday in April of that year. Health-wise, there hadn't been a massive deterioration and change, but he had lost interest in everyday activities and things he used to enjoy. It took such an amount of time and effort to try and get him to cook, something he had loved so much. His motivation had simply gone. In February 2016, he went to visit his doctor, Doctor Parr, for a routine diabetes check-up. For the first time, I didn't go in with Munnoo, as I thought there was no need and he knew and felt comfortable with Doctor Parr. I went off to a meeting and received a phone call advising me that Doctor Parr had decided that Munnoo required admittance to the hospital. It came as a shock, so I gathered some clothes for him and visited the ward. This was on the Friday, and when I arrived I just knew that Munnoo would not leave the hospital alive.

After taking the items in for him, I later returned home, allowing Munnoo to settle into the hospital. I wrote a message to the children, 'Dad's in hospital, doesn't look good.'

My eldest daughter, Ritu, arrived the very next morning from London. My younger daughter, Rachna, received the message whilst she was at work in India. She left work, booked a flight and arrived the next day. My son, Rohit, landed the following day. The children went to visit their father on their arrival. When my son got to the hospital, Munnoo said, 'Now that you have arrived, it's time to go.'

I can still see what happened in my mind, Munnoo holding his finger up and looking at Rohit as he said it. Then he stopped eating and drinking. He requested the nurses take his IV drip away. He had mental capacity and had made the decision that he wanted to die. Seeing his son had made him at peace with the finality of his death. In Hinduism, it is said that if your son performs your last rights, you will go to heaven. Whilst Munnoo did not practise his faith, such as going to the temple or praying, this was one thing that he did believe in.

Munnoo said his goodbyes to the children, which was important to him. When he passed, I wasn't there. I had been there for long hours, resting in a chair in the room, then I had returned home and my daughters were going to head to the hospital. Munnoo passed when I was at home, but Ritu and Rachna were there, as was Rohit. When I received the call from my daughter, I quickly made my way to the hospital. The nurses told me Munnoo had stopped breathing, that his heart had stopped. The doctor in me came out and I wanted to check for any signs of life. I didn't have my stethoscope on me, so instead I used the methods I had been trained in all those years ago by my teacher in India, of looking, touching and feeling for signs of life. I put my head to Munnoo's chest and, sure enough, there was no heartbeat. The doctors were then present to certify his death. It was hard, loss always is, and the loss of my life partner and father to my children was heartbreaking. However, it was a beautiful death in the fact my husband had his children around him, who he loved dearly. He wasn't in pain and he had the chance to say goodbye to us all, something many people are denied in death.

After Munnoo's death, we were inundated with support from the community. It meant a lot, just as Munnoo had meant a lot to South Shields. As time went on, the children were worried about me being in our large home, alone. It was three-bedroomed with lots of stairs. But it was my home and was filled with memories of my life here with Munnoo. My children wanted me to go back to India, but it was never up for consideration. I loved South Shields too much. This was home. The flats in Seymour Court became available, and although I originally wanted a two-bedroomed property, I bought a one-bedroomed flat here in May 2019. My children came and prepared the property for me, telling me I wasn't allowed to go there until they were finished!

I had no idea what they were doing, but then they announced it was ready. They had even prepared a ribbon for me to cut when entering the flat. Inside, they had assembled all my furniture, ensured all the photographs and memories were on the wall and made the flat comfortable and safe for me. It was lovely and their support really helped with the move, in particular the emotional shift from my old home to my new home. I am now, of course, very settled here and my neighbours are lovely. I have made many friends and the block has communal areas and events to bring all the residents together. I have the option to get involved with socialising, but I also have my own space and independence.

I enjoy keeping involved with the community and also having some rest time in my flat. I read a lot and watch murder mysteries on the TV. As well as this, I keep in touch with many friends, old and new. This helps me to keep active and manage my loss. I'm very grateful.

Both the men in my life, my father and Munnoo, made me the woman I am, and I am forever thankful for that.

60th wedding anniversary

Me and my lovely husband Munnoo (Triloki) on our 60th Anniversary in our back garden in South Shields

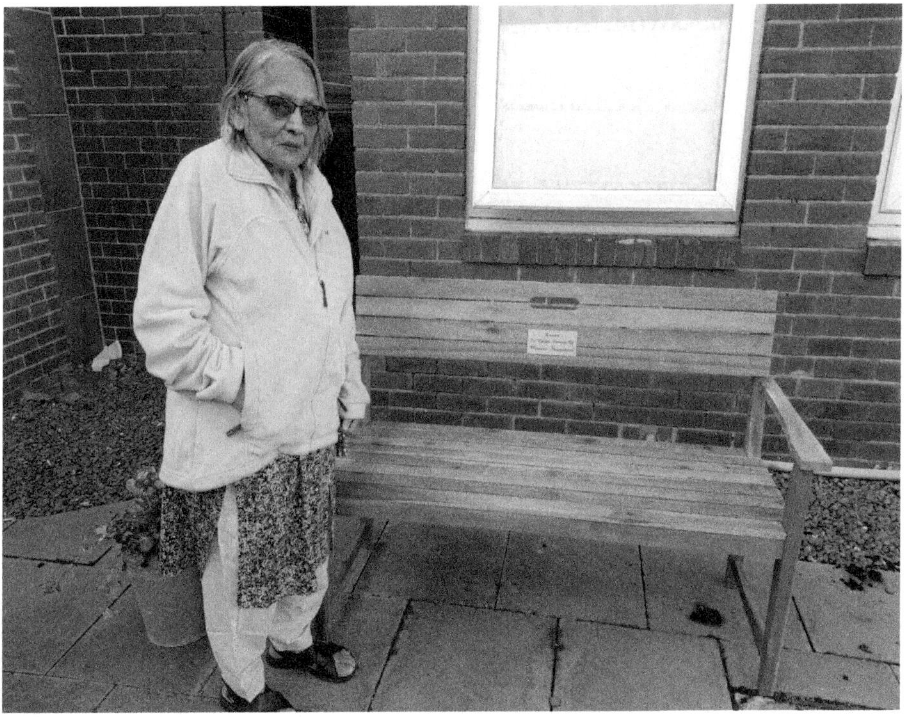

Donated to Ward 19 of South Shields District Hospital in memory of my husband, Munno for the love and care he received

On a recent visit to India - Feeling like a queen in the Royal Palki

6. LIFE LESSONS

My life has been long, with many experiences that I am grateful for.

I've been dedicated to my profession and my community. I wish others had this ethic and were committed to their craft and their community. People can make such an impact and difference when they have a strong work ethic. I have met some wonderful people in my life, in all the places I have lived, but especially in South Tyneside. Colleagues who have become friends, neighbours who have become friends and members of the community and all the groups I have been involved with have also become friends. I am fortunate to have met so many people and had so many opportunities. Life has been diverse, colourful and nourishing.

I have been blessed with my three children and my seven grandchildren. I'm very proud of them.

Life has not been without challenges, but I have always worked through this myself and with my family. In life, I learnt that trust in a relationship is essential. It was hard being away from Munnoo for so long, but he was faithful to me and loved me truly. We had trust and it was the foundation of our marriage. He did not have an easy time, being responsible for the children, with the help of my mother-in-law. He had to adapt to not being allowed to work in England after working hard in India. Over the years our roles changed, despite

Munnoo always wanting me to work and encouraging my development. I struggled in my career at times, through discrimination, but I kept going. I never gave up on my goals and dream.

I would hope that people reading this see that it can be done. When you set your mind to something and you embrace opportunity with a determined attitude, you can succeed. I am living proof of that. Achievement has been plentiful, as has the love we have shared as a family.

I hope I will be remembered for being hardworking, dedicated, sincere and genuine. For my dedication to the medical world and in particular my part in improving South Tyneside General Hospital. I also hope people will remember me for being a good friend and for being kind. People will recall my passion for the medical world, but also the community as a whole through my charity work and board member involvement in many organisations.

The most important quality in life is to be able to listen to people. This is essential in any career. In medicine, you have to listen to patients. This is when you find out the character of the person as well as any illness. Listening and not just hearing, as well as giving time to people, is important. Taking an interest in people and understanding them. These things really do matter and will assist anyone to go far in life, both in their career and outside of their career. Sometimes people want things as quick and easy as they can. For me, you work hard for what you have and you work hard to get better.

As my dad always said, 'There is nothing in the world you cannot do if you put your heart and soul into it. If you like what you do, you will be good at it.' I will never forget these important messages that have seen me through my life. I hope other people read this and will also believe they can achieve if they work hard, are determined and put their heart and soul into it.

Shobha the Environmentalist. Planted for the Queens Platinum Jubilee

Special Judges

People's Choice
Award
2021

abc
ASIAN BUSINESS CONNEXIONS
People's Choice
Award
2021
SPICE FM

With friends at Seymour Court

MBE, House of Lords

My adopted grandaughter